DEAD END DORCHESTER

VOL. 1

by Ses Carny

Illustrations by Kate Swanson

DED BOOKS
DEDBOOKS.COM

ISBN - 13: 978-1-7325561-0-2

Any similarities to historical events, real people, or real places are entirely coincidental. Names, characters, and places are products of the author's imagination.

Cover by Ses Carny.

Illustrations by Kate Swanson.

The author would like to thank Mr. Tony Gangi for all of the help that he provided in this publication.

Published and printed by DED Books, in the United States of America.

DedBooks.com

First printing edition - July, 2018.

Dead End Dorchester is a series of poetry and short story books, all based around a horror and thriller theme.

DeadEndDorchester.com

This book is dedicated to my little girl,
Molly. You are my whole world and
Daddy loves you, Babaloo.
Always.

(Molly's Zombie)

TABLE OF CONTENTS

INTRODUCTION

The first time that I ever made someone lose all control of their bodily functions was in 1993, when I was working for my very first haunted attraction. Oh, by the way, I was only 12 years old at the time. I have to smile to myself when I think about the fact that all of these years later I'm still doing what I can to scare the daylights out of people. There's just something about a gut wrenching scream (due to fun and frightful entertainment, of course) that can really get the blood pumping. Horror and Halloween are as much a part of my life, as is breathing.

I've always enjoyed telling stories, of virtually any nature, but it always seems to come back to horror. I think that is because Halloween was such a huge part of my life, growing up. Both of my parents loved Halloween and would try to get us kids (my brother, sister, and I) in on as much fun as they could. We were a hit with our classmates, because of the Halloween parties that our parents hosted.

We'd bob for apples, maybe watch a spooky old movie, and possibly go to a local haunted house. Without fail, we would always play this game that my Dad made up, in which he would put on an old latex werewolf mask and tie balloons to his ankles. The object of the game was to stomp on the balloons and pop them. To this day, I still have no idea of how many kicks he ever received from it, but I do know he had many large bruises after every Halloween party.

Most people have something that reminds them of their childhoods. A favorite movie, song, smell, book, etc... Something that takes them back to a magical time in their lives, filled with very fond and vivid memories.

For me, that "something" is the book "It's Halloween", by Jack Prelutsky and illustrated by Marylin Hafner, published in 1977. It's a collection of children's stories with a Halloween theme. When we were very young children, our aunt, Eileen (who lived with us), would read it to us now and again throughout the year, with regular nightly readings during October. I'll tell you, that book became such an integral part of my childhood, that I recently had all 4 of the main trick or treating characters tattooed on my right arm. My love of Halloween only grew from there, until the natural progression of life took me to the haunting business.

As of this writing, in 2018, I've been involved in the haunted house industry for 25 years. I've just about seen it all, when it comes to the vast array of ways to frighten people. I've played many different characters, with the majority being original ones that I've created.

To make a believable character, you must create a good back story for it, detailing who/what it is, where it came from, and any small details that can add to its past. In learning how to come up with those back stories, I also learned how to tell the story for maximum impact. My experience in the haunting industry, coupled with the handful of horror films that I have been in, I have a pretty good handle, I think, on what creates good scares that stick with you.

Am I a writer? Not really. I would consider myself more of a storyteller. I tend to write how I speak and my hope is that in doing so, it may help you in reading these stories around a campfire some night.

With the full moon rising overhead and just after the children have finished roasting their marshmallows, you will become the new storyteller by picking up this book and beginning to spin a web of both fear and fun.

Speaking slowly, you'll capture the attention and imagination of all of those who are listening. The flicker of the campfire flames will only help to cast shadows behind you that seem to dance in the trees. As you reach the end of each story, your voice has trickled to a soft, slow whisper. Your eyes widen gently, as you stare into the souls of each person within ear shot. Then, without warning, you jerk your head to the side and grab the first person nearest to you, while belting out an incredible scream.

If you want to see what true fear looks like, then try what I just described and you'll see it first hand.** Just make sure no one is eating or drinking anything as you do it. Remember, our goal is to scare them and then laugh it off - not to actually kill anyone. Just a heart murmur will do...

Enjoy, have fun, and most of all, I'd like to wish a very safe and Happy Halloween to you all!

~ Ses Carny

** If you do try to scare the *yell* out of everyone, I assume no responsibility for any deaths that may occur. So, on second thought, don't scare anyone. No scares equals no death and besides, funerals can be expensive these days.

Spooky Poems

THE DARKNESS

Sitting in the darkness,
With nothing much to do,

I can hear myself breathing
And I can hear you, too.

I hear you question why it is,
That it must be this way,

I want to tell you why it is,
Though I know I shouldn't say.

I hear you ask me how you died,
But I'll never be the teller.

For before you took your last breath,
You were buried in my cellar.

CRYING GIRL

There once was a girl who could not cry,

For if she did, she'd surely die.

She'd start to weep and stop the flow,

Always told not to let them go.

Then, one day, she dropped a tear,

It hit her cheek, but with no fear.

For it finally dawned inside her head,

She can cry all she wants, she's already dead.

FOOTSTEPS

Footsteps in the attic.
Footsteps in the hall.

Footsteps in the kitchen.
Footsteps that sound small.

Not the footsteps of my Mother.

Not the footsteps of my Dad.

Not the footsteps of my Brother.

But footsteps that sound sad.

Footsteps that are soft,
Like a scurrying little mouse,

The footsteps are from a ghastly ghost,
Who haunts our quiet house.

HAVE A HEART

Billy met Emma and it was love at first sight.
Only one thing was wrong,
In a world of all rights.

For Billy loved Emma,
More than words could say.
But Emma would not give her heart away.
She would not admit how she felt inside,
Until one day, when Billy died.

She was so sad; she just cried and cried.
Oh, how could it be that Billy had died?

About a week after his funeral, a box had arrived.
No marking from whom; what could be inside?
A note was found first upon opening the box,
Emma wasn't prepared to have quite a shock.
The note read, "I love you, I have from the start."
After looking inside, she found Billy's heart.

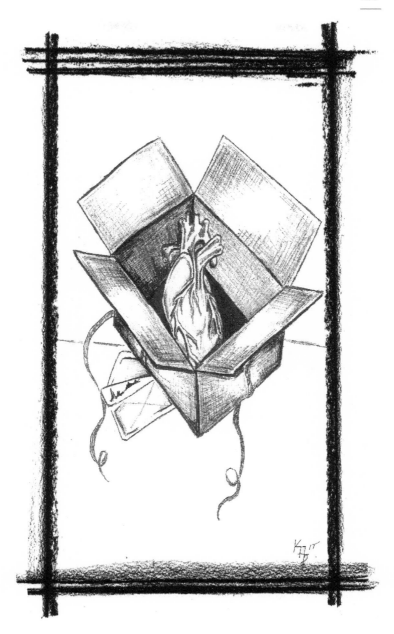

PALE ROSE

Born mute, without sound,
Born blind, without sight,
Born unable to tell,
The wrong from the right.

Kept from the world,
Hidden from light,
Her hair bleach blonde,
Her skin, bone white.

She only killed once,
Far as anyone knows,
When his blood touched her lips,
She became the pale rose.

WHISPERS

I hear whispers through the hallway,

Whispers up the stairs.

Whispers in the dining room,

Whispers that don't care.

They don't care if I hear them in the yard,

Or even by the bay.

They'll just keep on whispering,

Because the dead have a lot to say.

THE BRIDE

Donna died on her wedding night,
This left Michael very sad.

An illness struck that could not be stopped,
Yet Donna was still glad.

Glad for the time she had with Michael,
Glad for all they'd done.

She smiled as she slipped away;
Smiled after she was gone.

Michael heard her voice at night
And could smell her perfume, too.

He'd feel her hand touch his face while saying,
"I'm always with you."

THE BASKET

I once took a nap in a basket,

With a smell so bad, nothing could mask it.

Then with all of the rot inside my cot,

I remembered I'm still in my casket.

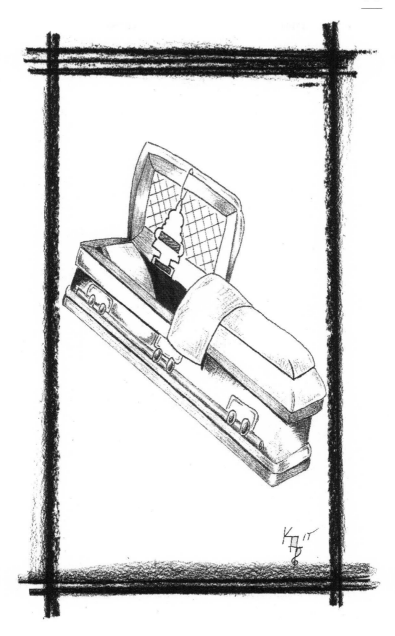

GHOST

There is a ghost down the hall,

He stands and stares and that is all.

He hardly says a single thing,

He doesn't talk, he doesn't sing.

He doesn't walk, he doesn't run,

He doesn't vanish in the sun.

There's only one thing we know he'll do,

If you get too close, he'll scream "BOO!"

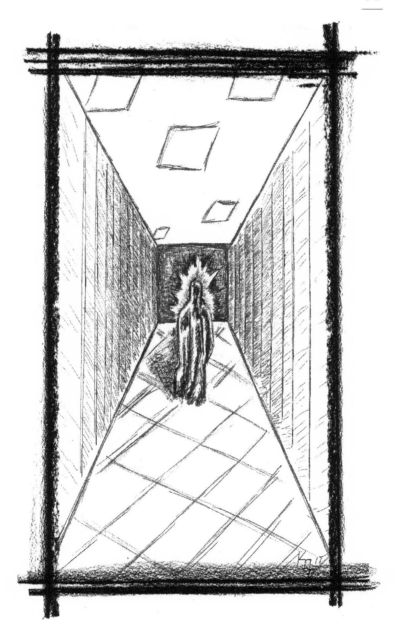

THE DOLL

Tori is a doll,
Just sitting, sitting, sitting...

She never seems to say a word,
Just grinning, grinning, grinning...

Then one night, as the moon shone bright,
I feared that I could see,

Tori was now standing and
She was staring straight at me

I watched her head turn slightly
And under my blankets I did dive,

For on that night,
When the moon shone bright,
I knew that Tori was alive

UNCLE TED

Johnny cried all night,
For he had a terrible fright.
His Uncle Ted, sat on his bed
And was quite a gruesome sight

Two years dead, was Uncle Ted,
There's no reason he should come.
Johnny was a frightened boy,
And the night was far from done

"Go! Go away, Uncle Ted!"
Johnny screamed from under the sheet.
Ted cracked a grin through his rotting face,
And said, "I will, but you're coming with me!"

THE DOG

Here I sit, broken-hearted,
I remember when it started.

A pet she wanted, so a dog she got,
A loving pet, it was not.

As she slept, one snowy night,
She woke up to quite a fright.

The dog, it sat upon her bed,
Growling madly, giving dread.

Eyes so red, they glowed like ember,
She knew right then, that cold December.

No matter how long she hid under fleece,
The dog would eat her, piece by piece.

JUST BREATHE

When you've fallen asleep in the bathtub,
Don't forget to breathe.

When you're swimming in the ocean and
The current pulls you far away from
The safety of the shore,
Don't forget to breathe.

When you fall off of a boat while fishing and
bump your head on the motor's propeller,
Don't forget to breathe.

When that piece of food gets
Caught in your throat,
Don't forget to breathe.

When you're lying in your casket,
You forgot to breathe

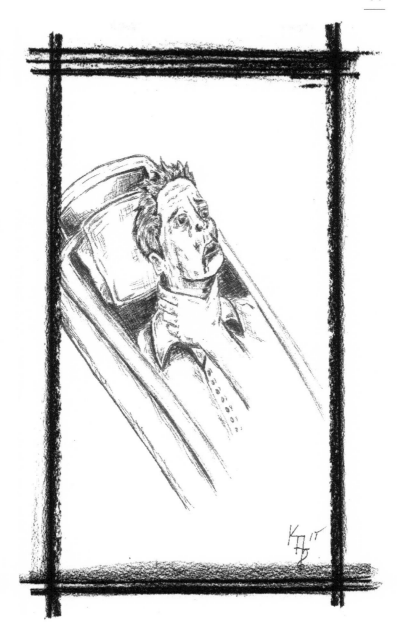

ECHOES FROM THE OLD OAK TREE

Come with me and you'll see,
The reason for my insanity.

I buried her, where no one could see,
Buried under the old oak tree.

Not in a crypt, no grave to see,
Buried under the old oak tree.

The wind breaks the silence,
On the moonless night.
Listen close and you can hear her plight.

Whispered songs of fear and fright,
Echoes off into the moonless night.

I loved her, oh how I loved her.
Sweet angels, here my cry!

She claimed to love me back,
But what then did I spy?

She wrote a note to a man,
My heart just broke right there.

I did for her all I could,
And this simply wasn't fair.

She had a voice as soft as clouds,
I thought could never lie,

But I knew she did not love me,
And surely had to die.

Sadly this was not the case,
As the mind is often wrong.

I found her letter addressed to *me*,
And it read like the calmest song.

Speaking in text of love and lust
And wanting to be wed,

I had not read this prior and now she's gone.
She's dead.

So I dug a hole deep enough,
To hide my secret deed.

Yet she reminds me in whispered song,
From beneath the old oak tree.

BETTY BOO-BOO

Betty Boo-Boo is her name,
A broken doll, not quite the same,
As the other dolls across the room,
Betty's fate was that of doom.

She was put upon the shelf,
Never to feel like herself,
For she was kept as a secret toy,
To never be seen by any girl or boy.

The problem is that she's not a doll,
She's not a toy, no not at all,
Her husband wouldn't give her up,
The illness couldn't stop his love,

She was once so full of life,
But now she's dead and a secret wife

HALLOWEEN

The sun has set, the moon is bright,
Let's see what sights we can see tonight.

Skeletons march row by row,
Ghosts and Goblins know where to go.
Devils, Witches, and Ghouls abound,
Jack-O-Lantern grins astound.

We watch as zombies shuffle on,
As crazy creatures have come and gone.
They all have a craving for just one thing,
Again, we hear the doorbell ring.

Superheroes, Aliens, Cowboys and more!
You never quite know what you'll have in store.
So many sights and monsters to meet,
When they all come, for our tricks or treats.

Creepy Tales

LEND A HAND

I was late for work. My first night on the new job and what sort of impression would this make? I had been home alone most of the day and should have laid out my work clothes earlier. I mean, it's just overnight demolition work, so I suppose jeans and a tee-shirt would be fine.

Reaching into the closet to grab a khaki button-down shirt to complete the look, I felt very uneasy. A feeling almost as if I were being watched. I grabbed the shirt from the coat hanger, but it was caught on something. Stretching in further, I could feel the tips of my fingers touch something.

And then I felt a hand touch mine.

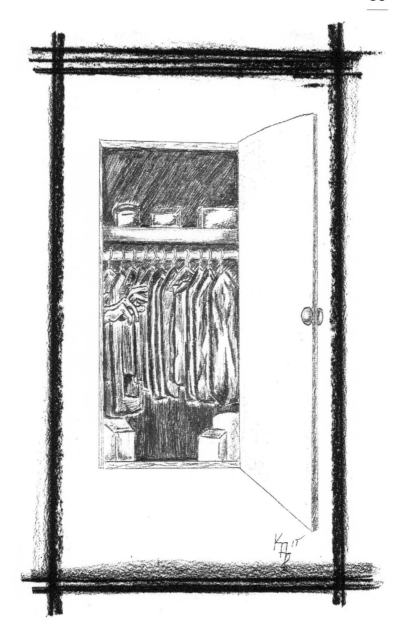

THE LITTLE GIRL

It's late and she's here again.

The little girl who stands at the end of my hall. Every Monday night she comes to stand there. Just stand there and cry.

I don't know exactly why she comes, except that the previous owners of the house had said that a little girl was murdered in that hallway.

So, every Monday she comes and every Monday she just stands there and cries.

One of these days I'm going to try and talk to her. One of these days... After I get over the fact that her face has rotted off.

MY BED

11:02pm

I've kicked off my boots from a rough day of work, have already had some dinner, and plan to watch a little T. V. before settling down for the night. All I want to do is get all cozy in my bed and watch a couple of reruns of shows that I like. Finally - time for some relaxation.

11:58pm

I just woke up to quite a startle. The television set was all white noise and static; it was pretty loud, too. I don't know what happened to the remote control, so I just get up to turn the set off manually. Stepping onto the floor, from my bed, there was an interesting sensation. As if the floor were refrigerated. It was very cold and had an odd smell coming from it. I thought it'd be best if I hurried along to get the T. V. set shut off.

11:59pm

I turned off the set and climbed back into bed.
While whistling away to myself, I heard
something odd, as if my whistle were softly
reverberated. It sounded as though it was coming
from... under my bed. Then I unmistakably
heard the sound of a giggle, as my bed suddenly
shifted.

12:00am

The bed shifted again and I could distinctly hear
the sound of heavy breathing coming from
underneath me. My only thoughts were that
someone had broken into my house and was
hiding under my bed! Suddenly I saw a hand
coming up from the side of the bed. Without
really thinking I grabbed it and just as I did, it
clutched back onto my wrist, pulling me out of
the bed and onto the floor.

12:01am

As soon as I hit the cold hardwood floor the hand let go of me, vanishing under my bed and I laid there in disbelief. Had I simply had a nightmare? Was I going crazy? As I stared under the bed I was completely shocked to see staring back at me... nothing, except for a few lost socks and some dust.

THE LIMOUSINE

A long black limousine drives slowly through the town, showing off the grandeur of the vehicle and the status symbol carried with it, that there must be a very important passenger inside. The only people riding in this coach are the driver, Mr. Manchetty, his aide, Mr. Lufkin, and the guest of honor who has the back of the car all to himself, Mr. Daniel Hayward.

"Oh yes, quite the honor it is, to be chauffeured around in such a unique car, for the entire town to see," Mr. Hayward kept thinking to himself.

There was only one problem. Where were they going? Mr. Hayward called out to Mr. Manchetty and Mr. Lufkin, however he was ignored. "Ah yes, the drivers aren't supposed to talk with the guests", Daniel seemed to recall from the time he had hired a limousine to take him to the theater.

For all he was worth, he could not remember where they were going, nor could he see where, due to the fact that he was blind. This didn't really bother him much at all because Mr. Hayward was determined to enjoy the ride, no matter what.

He could feel the limousine slow down and make a turn before, ever so slowly coming to a stop. He heard the front doors open and close and knew the drivers were about to open his door, finally letting him know where his final destination was. He heard another door open, that sounded as if it were behind him.

At that moment he came to the realization that he was not sitting in a seat, but rather laying down, confined and unable to move. Suddenly, he felt as though he was being pulled backwards and slowly he began to remember where they were headed and knew exactly where they were.

As the four strapping young men brought Mr. Hayward's casket into the light of day in the crowded cemetery, he thought, "Isn't this swell? I'm dead."

CREEPING CRAWLIES

Today seemed like a good day to try out my new insect repellent spray around the house. Boy, it sure worked like a charm. Those creepy little bugs scattered like crazy before they started dying. That meant I was finally going to get a good night's sleep without worry of ants getting into my boxes of cereal, slugs oozing up onto my bookcase or worse, spiders creeping on all eight hairy legs into my dresser drawer.

As I lay in bed trying to fall asleep, I distinctly felt something touch my hand. Sitting up, I leaned over to the small table next to the bed and turned on the lamp. Sure enough, there was a mosquito right where I felt something touch me. Slapping it with my other hand only served to splatter blood across my skin. The little pest must have been full from feasting on me.

Needless to say, I got out of bed and washed my hands well in my adjacent bathroom sink. Grabbing the hand towel off of the rack, I threw it quickly to floor after feeling something hard, that moved. The cloth hit the floor with such force that it knocked the hidden cockroach free from it's folds and the disgusting little disease runner scurried behind the toilet. Where in the world did a cockroach come from?

Back in bed and reaching for what I thought was the light switch, turned out to be nothing less than a large, hairy and slowly creeping spider! It was now on my hand and proceeded to bite me right where the mosquito had been sucking on my blood.

I screamed and promptly woke up, safe in my own bed. It was just a bad dream.

Throwing my blankets back so that I could get up to use the bathroom, I found that my entire bed was full of ants, roaches, worms and yes, even spiders, which were now rushing up into my open mouth, since I couldn't scream because of fear. They covered my face and were infesting my hair and ears, too. Gasping for air, I tried my best to pull them from my mouth, but more just kept coming. A spider crawled across my shock - induced open eyes and I felt every little step of each of its legs across my corneas.

I managed to let out a scream and once again, swiftly woke up. It was only a bad dream inside of a bad dream. That was a relief, until I reached under my blankets to make sure it was nothing more than just a nightmare and suddenly, I distinctly felt something slimy wiggle against my fingers.

SHIMMERING EYES

Letting out a long, tiresome yawn, I found myself no longer able to watch the TV. It didn't matter much anyhow. There's never anything good on lately; at least not at this hour and the scary movie that's on isn't really so scary. So, I got up out of bed, switched off the television and turned off the overhead light. Crawling back under the blankets, I began to think of the movie that was just on a few minutes ago. Monsters that hide in the dark? Where do they come up with this junk?

As I started to doze, I realized that I forgot to plug my phone in to charge. So I reached for it on the desk next to my bed, planning to use the light from the screen to see where the charging cable was. However, when I grabbed it, the screen felt wet. It almost felt like dog drool - sticky, slimy dog drool. But, I don't have a dog.

What the...? Confused, I turned the phone back on from its sleep mode. It had a nice soft glowing light coming off of the screen... and onto a set of shimmering eyes staring back at me.

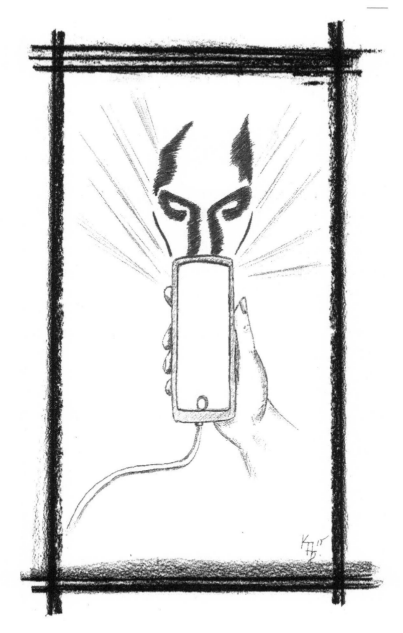

LOST

It was dark, somewhere around midnight, and I was very afraid; being lost in the forest had sent chills running up and down my spine.

Just when I was about to give up hope of ever finding my way out of the woods, a man appeared, offering to help me.

Was he possibly a fellow camper?

He said that he knew the way out of the forest and all I had to do was follow him.

By the moonlight, I could barely see him, but saw enough to make me ask myself, "Who is this man and why is he dressed like a clown?"

THE PETRIFIED WITCH'S HAND

My name is Gerald Goldstein (the surname given to my family upon immigrating to America) of Yuma, Arizona and the following statement that is presented within this document is, to the best of my knowledge, genuine in all accounts. The following story is retold here, as it was passed down within my family. For some, the piece of stone that is described herein may be nothing more than the broken hand of a statue, possibly from a weeping angel on a burial ground, however, I know it to be much more than that.

My twice Great-Grandfather, Father Bernard Gottschalk, was the (non-Prince Bishop) clergy for the Eichstätt territory in Germany, from the year 1623 through the year 1631.

During this time in history, there were many tragic witch hunts that broke out through the Early Roman Empire. Tragic, in that many of the accused were not witches at all, except for perhaps one.

Nina Fleischer was known for living on the outskirts of town, within the bordering forest, making her home in a small cabin that she herself built in the swamp. Rumors were vast and great, of her "treaties with the Devil", however no one dared to enter the dark swamp to confirm the suspicions of witchcraft. It was only when children in the town began vanishing that the political leaders of the territory felt that action had to be taken.

It was believed that no witch could harm a man of the church cloth, a clergy of God, and this is when my distant Grandfather was called in for aid. He was told to investigate Ms. Fleischer and to question her about the rumors that abound. As a safety precaution, he was given the presence of three other townsmen, should the need arise for help. The four men journeyed into the forest the next morning, after receiving their orders, with nothing more to protect them except my Grandfather's Bible, and a hand scythe carried by one of the other men.

After many hours of hiking, they came upon the swamp, finding the disheveled cabin, as they were told. My Grandfather offered a swift prayer for the men, as they traversed their way toward the wayward building. Reaching the cabin door and giving a brief knock, there was no sound to be heard, except the whimper of a small child from inside. Breaking down the door, the four men found the earthly remains of two children and one barely still alive, locked in a small cage.

At that moment, Nina Fleischer came forth from the loft of the cabin, propping herself directly on top of the cage which held the helpless boy. In a singular gesture with her right index finger touching his head, the boy instantly petrified into stone. With an evil laugh that my Grandfather said would haunt him for the remainder of his life; she lunged at the men, assuring them to receive the same fate as the boy.

In an instant of quick thought, my Grandfather held his Bible toward the crone, believing it to be a weapon against her evil magic. In a sinister counter, she touched her finger to the Holy book, causing it to also petrify into stone. He dropped the book just in time, before he too fell afoul of the creeping granite curse.

All of the men were frozen in fear, with no hope of stopping Nina. Slowly, she inched closer to one of the men, extending her finger, which was now obvious as the source of her wickedness. My Grandfather, once again in quick thought and more physical command, pried the hand scythe from the townsman next to him. Taking aim to the crone's hand and screaming so that God himself could hear his words, he shouted, "No more!", as he brought the scythe down with the force of the Heavens behind it, slicing through the wrist of the witch and severing her source of ill-gotten power. As she screamed with her last breathe, the severed hand, as well as the rest of her, petrified into stone. I suppose death mimics life.

Nina Fleischer was no more, nothing left except a statue. The hand was found on the floor of the cabin, frozen in stone in its ominous position, with three of the fingers broken off from its fall. My Grandfather lifted the pieces and gave them a blessing, praying for Nina's soul and that the black magic had been rid of her. He gave each one of the men a broken finger, instructing them to bury the pieces where no one might ever find them. He kept the remainder of the hand, offering a blessing to it daily, until his death in 1649.

He had aged only 56 years and upon his death, his wishes were for the hand to remain in our family ties and a daily prayer be said for it.

I know this story to be entirely true and not just because of the stone hand that I now possess. I have traveled to the very swamps where it all took place, deep in the forest of Eichstätt, Germany. It is there, in those forgotten swamps, that you can find one specific location that is slightly sunken in from where a small house, or cabin, once stood. When staring into the remains, you may still see the face of a statue, half buried in the muck. A screaming face. Nina's face.

I attest the previous to be whole and without falsification,

Gerald Goldstein

SPOOKY SIGHTS

It was Halloween night and I was sitting alone in the graveyard, enjoying the cool night air and taking in the spooky atmosphere. I nodded off and woke up to find three skeletons dancing around a small fire. The odd thing is that I wasn't even scared. They looked like they were having fun and didn't seem to notice me, which was fine since I was content being left alone to just watch.

Three large bats flew over my head, like giant rats with furry wings, flapping and squeaking in time with the dance steps of the bone troupe. I could hear cackling that sounded like it was right above me and looked up to the sky just in time to see two witches flying on their brooms, silhouetted by the full moon light. I closed my eyes in disbelief, only to awaken back in my own bed. Could it have just been a dream? No, because outside of my window, I could hear the cackling again and off in the distance I could see a fires glow coming from deep within the cemetery... I hope they're enjoying their Halloween party.

ACKNOWLEDGEMENTS

A very special thank you is extended to Charlie Urnick, for all of the support he has given over the years and the wonderful friendship he shares.

The author would like to thank the following individuals for their contributions toward the creation of Dead End Dorchester, Vol. 1. -

Laurie Richards, Laura Guimond, Nikky White, Ally Chilson, Marc Santosuosso, Erik DeNote, Jonathan Keith, Kim DeNote, Tricia Preble, Cathie Cabral, Paul LaChapelle, Daniel Robert, Christopher Galligan, Steven Wilson, Oli Elia, Megan Simpson, Nikki Virgin, Ed Vessella, Kristy Keane, Amy DeMoranville, Gail Ann Chandler, Kyle Cloutier, Pam Mueller, Donna Ruggieri, Tara Snearly, Brian Lawson, Pamela Flett, Ann Farrell (Oma Desala), Amara Rayne, Bruce Sullivan.

Thank you for helping to make a dream a reality.

ABOUT THE AUTHOR

Ses Carny is an American stage performer, actor, writer, and storyteller, currently based out of Boston, Massachusetts. He began his entertainment career at a very young age, performing magic shows in school for his fellow classmates. He would later go on to become a circus sideshow performer, crisscrossing all over America and Canada, entertaining at venues ranging from carnival lots and tattoo conventions to casinos and theme parks. You may have even seen him on television or in Ripley's Believe It Or Not.

His love for Halloween has always been forefront, though, playing a major role in his life. His family would dress up their home and yard with decorations for the holiday and then delight in frightening trick or treaters as they came to the door for their candy. Ses would help out in the "home haunt", terrifying kids and parents alike, ever since he was just ten years old. His entrance into the professional haunted house industry began just two years later.

Never looking back, "haunting" has also taken him around the country, scaring tens of thousands of patrons in the attractions that he has acted in. This also led to him being cast in several independent horror films, usually as some sort of monster characters. To say that Halloween is in his blood, is quite a literal statement, since his entire upper right arm is tattooed with a Halloween theme.

When not performing or scaring people, he enjoys writing, hiking, fishing, and most of all, spending as much time as possible with his daughter.

67781717R00054

Made in the USA
Middletown, DE
12 September 2019